# DOG PSALMS

DOG PSALMS
Prayers My Dogs Have Taught Me

Large-quantity purchases or custom editions of this book are available at a discount from the publisher. For more information, contact the sales department at Augsburg Fortress, Publishers, 1-800-328-4648, or write to: Sales Director, Augsburg Fortress, Publishers, P.O. Box 1209, Minneapolis, MN 55440-1209.

*Library of Congress Cataloging-in-Publication Data*
Brokering, Herbert F.
  Dog psalms : prayers my dogs have taught me / Herbert Brokering.
      p. cm.
  ISBN 0-8066-5160-1 (alk. paper)
  1. Dog owners—Prayer-books and devotions—English. I. Title.
  BV4596.A54B765 2004
  242--dc22          2004007847

Cover and book design by Michelle L. N. Cook
Cover and interior art from Artville

The paper used in this publication meets the minimum requirements of American National Standard for Information Sciences—Permanence of Paper for Printed Library Materials, ANSI Z329.48-1984. ♻ ™

Manufactured in the U.S.A.

HERBERT BROKERING

PRAYERS MY DOGS HAVE TAUGHT ME

# Dog Psalms

MINNEAPOLIS

Dedicated to dogs who have helped me pray:

Rex

Tippy

Peggy Ann

Scamper

Schnappsie

Spitz

Bruno

Millie

Blaise

# CONTENTS

# Introduction

I know dogs in my life the way I know people and cats and trees and landscapes. Dogs are in my mindscape and help shape my thoughts, feelings, and prayer life. Dogs have taught me attributes I feel in myself when reflecting and praying.

Dogs have shown me the spirit of being loyal, glad, overwhelmed, protective, committed, vigilant, patient, kind, energetic, discerning, forgiving. Unfolding these attributes of dog life opens my own spiritual being. My relationship with dogs mirrors my relationship with God. The title of this book might have been *God, I Am Dog*.

In *Dog Psalms* the reader can use a dog's attributes to speak to God. It is a natural connection. Like a dog, I, too, wait and watch. Waiting and watching is a silent power, a gift in me. I wait for what I want, hope for, long for, need. I wait for what is next, for company coming, a voice on the phone, a word from the doctor. I watch for those who are away.

God, I pray in my waiting and watching. You have given me the gift of time. You have told me later, tomorrow, next year, later, later, later. You are my good master.

Who are the dogs I have known best?

First, there was Rex, who lay in the sun with me on the |cellar door of our parsonage in rural Nebraska. Rex's thoughts were my thoughts, and his ways were mine. I knew every flea on his body seventy years ago, and I cared for him as my mother cared for me.

Tippy and Peggy Ann, spotted terriers, were mother and daughter. I braided them collars and harnesses. They were in my homemade circus, under a tent where I was most often alone, watching, marveling, in awe. This was a time before dog foods; Tippy and Peggy Ann ate our best scraps from the table. I cooked them porridge made of ground feed and wanted them to love it as I loved oatmeal.

There were highs of births, scampering puppies; there were lows of giving puppies away, saying goodbye, dog burials. Then came life in the city and new dogs from dog pounds, especially Scamper, a Japanese spaniel from Louisiana. I experienced the spirit of joy, wisdom, melancholy, faithfulness, and adoration inside with each new member of the family.

Schnappsie, a dachshund in Detroit, taught me to relax, wiggle, welcome, snuggle, stretch, sleep. A white spitz in the Haeckel parsonage taught me that dogs nip, yip, protect, and say, "This is mine," just as my siblings and I did at home. I saw Spitz and I saw myself.

Going to the Cronick home in Byron, Nebraska, was a high point. There was a bark of Bruno, a Newfoundland whose voice would have rung like an echo through the Swiss Alps. Each visit woke a dream in me to be a rescue dog in the mountains, searching for lost people and bringing them food and drink around my collar.

Millie is a dog who now visits hospitals and homes, walking corridors, greeting people in wheelchairs or on beds. She wears ribbons and hats and helps people smile who often lose their laughter. Some say she is an angel, some say a minister. Millie believes she is Dog.

*Dog Psalms* is about what dog lovers have learned from watching the best friend lying at their feet. These teachers wiggle and wag, snuggle, chase sticks, beg, depend on others for life, and exchange everything for lifelong commitments of faithfulness and love.

*Dog Psalms* is also about the human spirit, yours and mine. The readings are meant to help us speak out loud to our Master. We wiggle, we guard, we wait, we give, we hope, we hunt, we dig, we growl, we forgive, we beg, we stray, we whine, we jump, we snoop, we cuddle, we nudge, we pant, we charm, we heal. And our Master watches and loves us through it all.

*Herbert Brokering*

Herbert Brokering

## J trust.

***I am dog.*** *I am loyal.*

*Your trust is in me. You help me grow my trust. More and more we belong to each other. I pledge allegiance to you, as you have to me. When you double your faithfulness to me, I triple mine to you. I lean on you when I cannot stand by myself. When you have need, I will hold you. I am willing to help and to be helped. Your trust grows my loyalty. I depend on your dependability. Trust was planted in me long ago in the womb. Our trust will have no end. I depend on your kindness for a good life. I am dog and I am loyal. I need your faith for my faith.*

**God,**

You have given me your trust. Loyalty is in me. I am yours as you are mine. In a storm, I lean on you and you hold me. You are my anchor; in doubt you are my hope. There is no clear line between us to keep us apart. You surround me and are inside me. You are above and below and beside me. Your faithfulness gives me faith.

# ꭺ wiggle.

*I am dog.* *I love you.*
*My whole being shows*
*you my affection. With*
*eyes and lips and paws*
*and tongue, I love you. I*
*assume with my whole self*
*that you love me too. I wiggle and wag and jump and climb and*
*pant for you to love me. I am dog. I feel innocent even after proven*
*guilty. I love you unconditionally, believing you love me the same. I*
*am dog. The tides of the oceans are in me. I wiggle as I ride waves,*
*hear love calls of ancient forests, feel the kiss of a wisp of wind. I*
*have a spirit that runs through all times.*

**God,**

My spirit wiggles in me. I dance in my heart when I feel your closeness. I cannot hold my feelings still. Your spirit runs through me like a living stream, a slow rhythm, and with you I am young. You keep me alive with goodness from the earth and the heavens. You find the good in me. You move me with your joy.

# I plead.

*I am dog. My eyes sometimes look far away, search skies, sweep the horizon.*

*My eyes sometimes look to you, inside of you, through you. With my eyes I plead. My eyes meet your eyes and hold you, fix you, ask you, capture you. My heart can wrap around your heart so you can see my need, my want, my hope. Then I am in your heart. I can stare into your spirit. The deep silence in my eyes is stronger than my bark. I can bury my eyes in your eyes until we find tears. I can plead until you out plead me. We hold each other in our eyes.*

**God,**

You see me plead with all my heart. I beg and do not hold back. I want, I wish, I need, I hope in front of you. I am careless in asking favors. I bury myself in you while you hold me in your eyes. I fix my thoughts on you until you capture me, quiet me, silence me. Your loving silence and touch hold me still.

## I skip.

*I am dog. I can flood with emotion, fill with sudden happiness.*

*I tremble with affection when you come home early. If I am asleep when you come, I stretch, skip, hurry, feel more awake than ever. My body is filled with power. I am ready to go; I run, leap, swim. I am sometimes overwhelmed. I run in circles, jump, bark. I can be so overwhelmed I leap into you, believing you will catch me, hold me, pet me, love me. When you surprise me, I can run faster to you than I ever ran, without even trying. I am dog and I overwhelm. I have no control over the spirit of my fullness.*

**God,**

My spirit runs in circles. Sometimes I fly, I climb, I flee. I go places beyond my daily life. I soar to heights eagles cannot ascend. I run races too fast for runners. I see beauty never painted, hear harmonies never written. I am a child who skips with my heart. You fill my life to the brim.

# I guard.

**I am dog.** *I protect.*

*I know what is mine and yours. If it is yours it is like mine and I will guard it with my bark, my bite, my growl, myself. I will protect what I treasure with my whole being. My hair will stand on end, my body stiffen, my legs stretch strong, my eyes lock on what seems to be the enemy. I will judge the distance between the enemy and me; my voice will dictate the boundary I determine. If the enemy crosses my line, I will leap into a war dance meant to frighten. The dancing also makes me feel safe. I will lay down my life for what I strongly believe. I am dog. I protect.*

**God,**

I keep up my guard. I say what is mine and I draw a fence around it. I protect what is precious to me. To guard and keep it safe, I raise my voice to make myself bigger than I am. I study boundaries that keep safe what is special. Show me the source of all my strength. Remind me who guards me and who sees me as precious. Then teach me how I am to defend.

# I commit.

*I am dog. I believe in unconditional love.*

*I do not settle for infatuation or puppy love. I believe in true love to the end. I am a life-long lover who will lie at your feet, on the bed, by your chair, at your side. I am dog. I insist on your love. I will stay on a grave of a lover until my end. I believe in commitment. When we have chosen each other, I will be there for you, with plenty. Out of my heart flows life and love. You fill my life with abundance and I am fulfilled. Unconditional love is the highest gift. I am committed to love.*

**God,**

You gave me your love before I met you. You do not hold back or tease me with what you give. I am learning the strength of your unconditional love. You have shown me your commitment throughout my life; you have committed to me beyond this life. You have promised me love I cannot comprehend. You have made me a committed believer in commitment.

# I watch.

*I am dog.* *I am vigilant.*
*I watch with my eyes*
*shut. I wake while I sleep.*
*If a room is ours, I will*
*keep it safe. If it is our*

*yard, I will watch all four corners. Sometimes my vigilance is*
*greater than my body weight, swifter than my leap. Sometimes my*
*vigilance shrinks to a whimper, whisper, silence. Yet I am there, and*
*being there is also my vigilance. I will not flee readily. One growl*
*and the enemy fears. One stir and the enemy steps back. I show my*
*teeth and the enemy is sure I bite. I lift my head, I rise; the enemy*
*runs away. I am a force, ready to prove my strength. I am dog. I*
*wake quickly, vigilant. I watch out for you even when I rest.*

**God,**

I am vigilant even when my eyes are closed. I listen even
when there is no sound. I look when there is nothing in sight.
I keep watch with you. I wake quickly where there is need and
will hurry to help without being told. I am vigilant, ready to
stand or flee. I run in the dark and know where to find help.
You do not leave me alone. I am ready to go, for you are
already there.

# I wait.

**I am dog.** *I am patient.*
*I can be taught to wait. I do not
prefer to wait in a long line; I want
to be the only dog waiting. If you
are coming, I will wait, breathing
deeply, half dreaming, wholly wishing. When I know you love me, I
live for you with every breath. I bury my yearning deep inside and
hide it in my sleeplessness. I toss and turn and wait until you are
here. I wait for you sometimes while singing, sometimes while
whimpering, howling, wanting with all my heart. I can wait loud
or soft. I can wait through long night watches. I will wait without
end, knowing I am wanted. I am dog, willing, patient. Waiting
prepares me for your presence.*

**God,**

You have given me the gift of waiting. Like a child, I wait with my whole body, mind, and soul. I wait for seasons, they go; I wait for another, it comes. I wait for days to dawn, nights to darken, seeds to break open, fruit to fall. As I wait I learn the gift of patience and the joy of surprise. While I wait I find myself in your presence. I wait for you, and in waiting I see you are here, waiting.

# I give.

*I am dog.* I am kind. When you come home, I will give you my full attention. I will give you my place, my time, my whole day, myself. While you heal, I will comfort, lick your hand, be still, stay near you. If you need, I will give you a night watch. I will be glad when you are glad, run when you run, leap when you leap. I want to be with you, see your laughter, feel your kindness. When you give abundantly, I think of thanks. See how I gulp the food you give, lap the cool drink, come running before you finish calling me? I want you to witness my acts of kindness. My kindest word is in my deed.

**God,**

I am thankful for the wonder of giving. I know the feeling of breaking a cookie in two to share it, of wrapping something ordinary with a bow, of handing on a good story as legacy, of dividing my time with another. Your loving kindness is in me, and I will do acts of mercy I do not plan. Your giving is becoming a habit in me. I am learning kindness.

# I hope.

*I am dog.* *I expect a treat. It is not that I always deserve, but I expect a treat, a hug, a pat, a good word, a compliment. I expect you to treat me like the dog I truly am, the dog inside me who is even greater than the one people know. The dog inside is more loyal, more watchful, more playful than some have seen me. You make me feel worthy of a treat; you are the one who spoils me, satisfies me, makes me expectant, hopeful. You have taught me to expect my just reward. You want me to be treated to a treat. I receive over and over. I am full of hope from head to toe.*

**God,**

The gift of hope is built into my world. There are paths and windows and doors open to what is coming. You have taught me to expect and wish and ask and hope. You give to me over and over and over, so I know there is more and more. Hope is at the edge of each night and day, each season and place. As a bloom is in the seed, so your hope is stored in me. Unfold the hope in me.

# I laugh.

**I am dog.** *I am ready to be happy.*

*I am designed to wag, smile, laugh, radiate joy. A glance, a touch, a morsel, a whistle, and I feel the good run through me. Take me for a walk or run, save me from the cold, be near me, play with me, and I will be glad. I can show my delight with a shiver, a closing of my eyes, a single bark. Those who love me know the moment I shine, grin, laugh out loud. I can save my joy, hold it in; it can explode, knock you down. One tiny word, one wink, one hug can make me happy all day. I am glad for simple things. Inside me is a feeling waiting to laugh.*

**God,**

You make us laugh. Creation is full of joy. The sea and earth and heavens rejoice. There is a humor on earth that we catch, and so we laugh and tease and are glad. We wink and smile and whistle and bend over laughing. There is a joy in us we cannot contain. Fun breaks out; shouts and barks and meows and warbles explode. You give us comedies and anthems and parades and celebrations. You have created life with a strong sense of laughter.

# I hunt.

*I am dog.* *I was born to hunt.*

*I sniff the ground, the air, the wind, the*

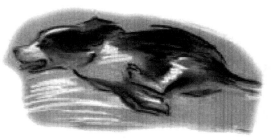

*sky, the familiar, the new. I watch the horizon, the brush, the leaves to know what moves. I am predator of rabbits, squirrels, raccoons, ducks, bees, or bits of table food. I hunt what is near and what I never ever find, which sleeps like a dangling carrot inside my ancestry. I will trace sounds you cannot hear, smells you cannot smell, sights that are specks in the sky. I will follow the trail for miles. I was born in the wild but trained to repress, bred to repress. I am always on the hunt. I follow the Geiger counter inside me. I am dog. I know my target.*

**God,**

I hunt what I never find. I seek what I never see. I am on the go, looking, digging, uncovering. You take me where I have never been, and I return to places as though I have not seen them before. My world stays new; there is a vista before me, and then another. I come to one horizon and there is the next. Inside me is an eye that needs to seek and find what is hidden before me.

# J chase.

*I am dog. I chase.*
*I chase to catch, to*
*win, to conquer. My eye*
*will not leave the chase. I*
*will spin, jump, climb, dig,*
*sprint in pursuit. I am*
*made to chase. I chase to play. I snatch balls in mid air, dive after*
*sticks in deep water, twist and soar to capture Frisbees. If no one will*
*throw for me, I will chase my tail, my shadow. I will snap at the*
*wind, a falling autumn leaf, snow in flight. But I chase best with a*
*friend, an audience, someone cheering, shouting my name. They*
*know I am chasing, chasing, chasing. I am dog. I have goals to*
*catch.*

**God,**

My spirit is on a chase. I run through meadows into summer wind, follow clouds fast on the move, reach to catch a dancing snowflake, look up at migrant flights, and follow a tumbling leaf to the ground. There are paths I run to find a rising sun, streets I walk to meet the same friends, prayers I say each day, and words I read again and again and again. I chase old and new routes and know when I have caught what I am hunting. I have chosen what it is I chase most.

# I dig.

**I am dog.** *I am filled with curiosity.*

*I want to know what is not my business. I dig. I plow under leaves, poke through a toy box, and route out a clump of rags to find the spirit of what is not there. Without any excuse, I ravage a tiny earth hole where there is neither mouse nor bird nor chipmunk in hiding. I am eager to discover what has long been gone, save the scent. I can test a spider from more sides with my paws than Picasso could with a brush. When something is just out of reach, I am overcome with a wanting spirit. I will return again and again until my curiosity is satisfied. My need to seek and find is relentless. I have an inquiring spirit.*

**God,**

I dig. I want to know. You have made me curious. I want to learn more. I want to know the sky by heart, know the planets by name and point them out to my friends. I want to learn another language to hear the thoughts inside other people. Thank you for those who discover what has long disappeared, which we need to know. Give me the mind to stay with things that are important, so I find their meaning and beauty.

# I growl.

*I am dog. I growl.*
*I growl to possess,*
*to protect, to ward*
*off, to own. Growling is my act of diplomacy. It is my warning,*
*my first signal of danger ahead, my good will. I growl to stop*
*confrontation so I need not bite. My growl is greater than my anger.*
*With it, I create the distance I need between us. Growling is often*
*as far as I go with harm and defense. After growling I am known to*
*run off, hide, duck, or wag as an alternative approach. In growling,*
*I test the danger, estimate the harm, interface with foe or friend.*
*Growling is my checkpoint. I am diplomat, I measure respect, I*
*watch over peace. I am an ambassador for good will.*

**God,**

I growl. I growl to ward off danger; my growl is a shield around me. I growl to create a distance that makes me safe. My growl gives me a little time to understand what I am to do next. I do not want the fight; I want the peace. Move me quickly from growling to grace, turn my confrontation into good will. Make me an ambassador of understanding.

# I shine.

*I am dog.* *I am bred. My lineage is celebrated. I am known for my teeth, called by a Latin name. People study my pedigree, compare me with ancestors, consider my descendants. I may have a lineage that begins in China or Germany. I may be famous for mixtures some call Heinz. Pictures of my kind are colored by school children, published in books. I look like breeds before me. Yet with my distinctiveness, I win blue ribbons. I am created after my own kind. In my family are traits hunters want, children love, shepherds buy, police train. I am made to be fierce, coy, shy, swift, gentle, strong, sweet. I have a mold not easily broken. I am dog. I have a lineage. My character is built for greatness.*

**God,**

I have a pedigree. I have value. I am somebody. People know me a certain way. Yet I am like no one else. There is a lineage I own that is my own. My traits qualify me for a lifelong work. People want me for who I am, how I feel and act, what I am able to do. Unfold in me the lineage I have inherited that makes me special. Help me to be what I am to be. I am glad to have my life.

# I work.

*I am dog. It is my nature to work.*

*I can guard property, guide sheep, attack foes, find wrongdoers, point out fowl, jump through hoops. I am good at my work. I am happy when visiting sick, walking from old to young, wagging, snuggling, schmoozing, getting treats. I live for pulling sleds through snow, corralling scattered sheep in valleys, finding survivors in rubble. My nature is to work. You will know me by my good work. I am at my best when on duty. You need me. I am worth my bread.*

**God,**

There is business to do in the world, and I will do some of the work. There are loads to pull, burdens to hold, sick to heal, rivers to forge. Here I am; I am worth my bread. There are lost to find, races to win, people to cheer, poor to feed. There is business to do in the world; some of the work is mine. Show me the work I am able to do. Guide me when I volunteer.

## I miss.

*I am dog.* I miss you.

If you are gone too long, I grow listless and lose my glow. I feel shaggy inside. When I finally see you, I run to meet you more than halfway. I overwhelm you with my signs of missing you. Missing you stores a power in me that explodes in your presence. If I am old, I act young again. If I hurt, I feel no pain. If I am weak, I grow strong again. As I miss you, I prepare to give you everything I am, in a flashing moment. I miss you the way I think you miss me. I do not ask how much you miss me; I believe how much you miss me.

**God,**

I long for someone. I miss people. I miss those I knew and will not see. I miss those I know and are not here. I miss some I have never met. I miss some before they leave me. I miss the places I know by heart, every aroma, every tree, every flower, every nook and cranny. You have made me with the gift to miss, to long for, to stay connected to what is never finished. When I miss, I feel a great power leaving. I wait for its return, and then I will dance.

# I forgive.

*I am dog. I forgive without asking for forgiveness.*

*I will forgive before you are ready to receive my look, my lick on your hand. I do not bargain forgiveness; I do not make a deal. You are forgiven even before you harm or holler or neglect or ignore. Tomorrow is a new day. Tonight is already a new time. The sun will not set on my anger. I forgive you for I am yours and you are mine. We agreed without a signed document. You can hold me to words I cannot say, to a sentence I cannot write. Hold me to who I am. I am dog and I forgive. Forgiving feels right. I do not ask why. I will not sleep with a grudge.*

**God,**

I forgive. I will not go to sleep with a grudge. I do not carry anger with me for long. I know the strength and peace inside forgiving. I believe forgiveness weakens a battle line, erases wrinkles in the spirit, brings relief to my mind. I forgive and chains fall, foe becomes a friend, a family relaxes, children hug and sing and play again. Forgiveness makes possible change, a time to grow, telling the truth, acts of kindness, reconciliation. Your forgiveness is in me.

# I stray.

**I am dog.** I stray.

I follow what I want for a while, then lose where I am and what I was seeking. I wander off the path we walk each day, then make a bend that is new. If I cannot find my way back, you worry. You hunt for me. You post my name and picture and offer a high reward. Lost, I tear myself apart. Sometimes I run in frantic circles. I share the hurt of being lost. I am sorry that I stray, yet once found, I may stray again. You know I may stray again. I will listen for and hear your call. I am dog. I wait to be found. I will go far to be with you again.

**God,**

You hunt me and find me when I stray. You know every turn I make, what I wander off to see, and when I am lost and cannot find home. You call my name and I hear your voice. If I am frantic, your voice does not leave me. You give laughter to loved ones when I return. So there is joy in the universe, and heavens, when something lost is restored. How is that you give us the gift to wander so?

# ♩ nest.

**I am dog.** *I nest.*

*I turn and turn to lie down. I know the basket, the rug, the corner, the couch. I make the place my safe nest. I nest like a bird, making sure my place is right. I nest where I can see you, feel you near, hear your voice, guard you. I nest in a ritual of comfort, knowing I am now home. My nest is mine, found and prepared through time. It is our place. The light is right, the mood is right, the spirit right, so I lay me down to rest. I nest, and all around me there is certain peace. I turn, lie down, I enter into your presence. This is our place.*

**God,**

I know my place of rest. It is our place, where I hear you best, where you are near and I am safe. You give me places that are my home, where my spirit is right, mind is right, mood is right. You see me turn this way and that way, inside, outside, until I find my nesting place. In all sounds and sights around and within, you show me how to stay where I am to find your presence. Thank you for our still places, they are holy.

# I snuggle.

*I am dog.* I snuggle.

I get close. I snuggle
into your body, under your
arms, into your lap,
between your feet. I snuggle in your bed, into your eyes, into your
presence. I snuggle into your voice, into you favorite chair, behind
your pillow, beneath your book. I wrap myself around your heart. I
am created to be close to you, with you, of you. I can snuggle so we
are like one. When I move, you move. I sleep then you sleep. You
wake then I wake. You stretch, I stretch. I snuggle to stay near
when we are apart. You are more near than far. I feel your snuggle
when you are away. I am absolutely loved.

**God,**

I snuggle. I get close, stay near, get deep into your presence. I look for your words that make me safe, keep me close, love me. I look for your heart in all words and stories. I want your presence wrapped around me. You show me your way, and I want to walk that way. When I see how far the universe is spread, I want to be close. I want to be under your arms, in your hands, and at your feet. You are more near than far.

# ꙇ bluff.

*I am dog. I bluff,
and I am good at it.
Though I may be
small, I can make my
bark far bigger than my bite. The situation determines the size of
my bluff. I bluff to get attention. I bluff as a first line of defense. I
am usually better at fencing than fighting. I use a bluff to talk to
strangers, to know why they came, if they can be trusted. A bluff is
like a peephole in a door, a safety chain before I open wide. A dog
likes to know who is asking to come in. If I bluff the same people
over and over, they will not believe me. I do not bluff those I trust
most. I am dog. I am honest. I need truth to set me free.*

**God,**

I bluff. My bark is bigger than my bite. My bluff is the way I
negotiate. My spirit fences. My spirit weighs my strength in
the presence of what is new. I am cautious before I open
myself to what I have never seen. I test the ice before I walk
into the middle of everything. I bluff to find out where we
stand, so we can talk. You make me grounded. I do not bite
and will not fight. I am learning to trust.

# I nudge.

*I am dog.* *I nudge.*

*I look to you for abundance, for more and more and more. I dig my nose into your hands. I know where to push so you feel the power of my nudge. When your hand is empty, I do not show disappointment. I stay to receive what I think is there for me. I stay so you feel my hope grow. I nudge to dream of what more you have. I can tell when the nudge is welcomed. I nudge and stay so you can nudge me back. To be close is often enough. Your presence is my peace. My nudge is a wish that you have heard me. When you nudge back, then I am in you. I am dog. I nudge, I receive. I am contented. I am at rest.*

**God,**

Stay close. You know I need more and more of what you give. I dig myself into your presence until I feel you hold me. I look for your promises. I bury myself into your mercy and might. You touch me, and I touch you back. Your presence is my peace. I nudge you, I find the palm of your hand, I am contented. You are here for me.

# I pant.

*I am dog. I pant.*

*I pant when the sun is hot. I pant when I have run hard. I pant after a chase to catch what is thrown for me. I lay down at your feet a winner, exhausted. I pant for coolness, fresh water. I pant, I crave, I long violently for the mystery of life. I come to the water and drink. Throw me into the summer water and I come back to you, soaked, shaking myself dry. I am dog. I crave. I look to you. I am quenched. My heart is refreshed. My thirst is satisfied.*

**God,**

My soul pants for living water. I go through desert places and I thirst. I feel the coolness of a running stream, and I am refreshed and made glad. I lay me down beside still waters. My soul is restored. I yearn and I thirst for a drink that quenches my hunger, and I am satisfied. In your water I find life.

# I heal.

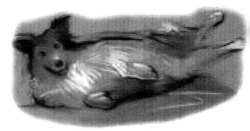

*I am dog. I make well.*

*People tie a ribbon on me; they feel better. I wear a sweater, a jacket, a bonnet; children laugh and lose their pain. I catch a Frisbee; voices cheer me on. I roll over; crowds gather in awe. People give me compliments I do not understand, but I feel their words. Ones I love take me to visit people who are alone. We walk down corridors in a healing parade. I snuggle with sick from bed to bed. All ages kiss me, look me in the eye, tell me what they cannot say to each other. I know their souls, their hurt, their fear. I know the bark they need to hear. When people hold me, they are better than before. When I leave, people wave. We bless each other. I smile. I am dog, I am here to make well.*

**God,**

You bless me so I bless. You make me your own, and I carry your goodwill into the world. I have places where I go door-to-door, bed-to-bed, sick-to-sick. I bring good news, a smile, a touch, understanding, a flower, empathy. They are glad when I come. We pray. They wave when I leave. But it is not over. They wait and I return. I stay with them, and they with me, while we are apart. You give us this gift of real presence. I am here to be well.